T0164941

Userid/Password Address Book

Stores all of those userids and passwords
you have written on scrap paper all in one
handy address book!

Lori Cunningham

BALBOA.
PRESS
A DIVISION OF HAY HOUSE

Copyright © 2011 Lori Cunningham

All rights reserved. No part of this book may be used or reproduced by any means, graphic, electronic, or mechanical, including photocopying, recording, taping or by any information storage retrieval system without the written permission of the publisher except in the case of brief quotations embodied in critical articles and reviews.

ISBN: 978-1-4525-3774-0 (sc)
ISBN: 978-1-4525-3775-7 (hc)

Library of Congress Control Number: 2011914508

Balboa Press books may be ordered through booksellers or by contacting:

Balboa Press
A Division of Hay House
1663 Liberty Drive
Bloomington, IN 47403
www.balboapress.com
1-(877) 407-4847

Because of the dynamic nature of the Internet, any web addresses or links contained in this book may have changed since publication and may no longer be valid. The views expressed in this work are solely those of the author and do not necessarily reflect the views of the publisher, and the publisher hereby disclaims any responsibility for them.

The author of this book does not dispense medical advice or prescribe the use of any technique as a form of treatment for physical, emotional, or medical problems without the advice of a physician, either directly or indirectly. The intent of the author is only to offer information of a general nature to help you in your quest for emotional and spiritual well-being. In the event you use any of the information in this book for yourself, which is your constitutional right, the author and the publisher assume no responsibility for your actions.

Any people depicted in stock imagery provided by Thinkstock are models, and such images are being used for illustrative purposes only.
Certain stock imagery © Thinkstock.

Printed in the United States of America

Balboa Press rev. date: 08/24/2011

Companies/Businesses

Company/Store name: _____
Website: _____
Userid: _____
Password: _____

Company/Store name: _____
Website: _____
Userid: _____
Password: _____

Company/Store name: _____
Website: _____
Userid: _____
Password: _____

Company/Store name: _____
Website: _____
Userid: _____
Password: _____

Company/Store name: _____
Website: _____
Userid: _____
Password: _____

Company/Store name: _____
Website: _____
Userid: _____
Password: _____

Companies/Businesses A

Company/Store name: _____
Website: _____
Userid: _____
Password: _____

Company/Store name: _____
Website: _____
Userid: _____
Password: _____

Company/Store name: _____
Website: _____
Userid: _____
Password: _____

Company/Store name: _____
Website: _____
Userid: _____
Password: _____

Company/Store name: _____
Website: _____
Userid: _____
Password: _____

Company/Store name: _____
Website: _____
Userid: _____
Password: _____

Companies/Businesses

Company/Store name: _____
Website: _____
Userid: _____
Password: _____

Company/Store name: _____
Website: _____
Userid: _____
Password: _____

Company/Store name: _____
Website: _____
Userid: _____
Password: _____

Company/Store name: _____
Website: _____
Userid: _____
Password: _____

Company/Store name: _____
Website: _____
Userid: _____
Password: _____

Company/Store name: _____
Website: _____
Userid: _____
Password: _____

Companies/Businesses

Company/Store name: _____
Website: _____
Userid: _____
Password: _____

Company/Store name: _____
Website: _____
Userid: _____
Password: _____

Company/Store name: _____
Website: _____
Userid: _____
Password: _____

Company/Store name: _____
Website: _____
Userid: _____
Password: _____

Company/Store name: _____
Website: _____
Userid: _____
Password: _____

Company/Store name: _____
Website: _____
Userid: _____
Password: _____

Companies/Businesses

Company/Store name: _____
Website: _____
Userid: _____
Password: _____

Company/Store name: _____
Website: _____
Userid: _____
Password: _____

Company/Store name: _____
Website: _____
Userid: _____
Password: _____

Company/Store name: _____
Website: _____
Userid: _____
Password: _____

Company/Store name: _____
Website: _____
Userid: _____
Password: _____

Company/Store name: _____
Website: _____
Userid: _____
Password: _____

Companies/Businesses

Company/Store name: _____
Website: _____
Userid: _____
Password: _____

Company/Store name: _____
Website: _____
Userid: _____
Password: _____

Company/Store name: _____
Website: _____
Userid: _____
Password: _____

Company/Store name: _____
Website: _____
Userid: _____
Password: _____

Company/Store name: _____
Website: _____
Userid: _____
Password: _____

Company/Store name: _____
Website: _____
Userid: _____
Password: _____

Companies/Businesses

Company/Store name: _____
Website: _____
Userid: _____
Password: _____

Company/Store name: _____
Website: _____
Userid: _____
Password: _____

Company/Store name: _____
Website: _____
Userid: _____
Password: _____

Company/Store name: _____
Website: _____
Userid: _____
Password: _____

Company/Store name: _____
Website: _____
Userid: _____
Password: _____

Company/Store name: _____
Website: _____
Userid: _____
Password: _____

Companies/Businesses

Company/Store name: _____
Website: _____
Userid: _____
Password: _____

Company/Store name: _____
Website: _____
Userid: _____
Password: _____

Company/Store name: _____
Website: _____
Userid: _____
Password: _____

Company/Store name: _____
Website: _____
Userid: _____
Password: _____

Company/Store name: _____
Website: _____
Userid: _____
Password: _____

Company/Store name: _____
Website: _____
Userid: _____
Password: _____

Companies/Businesses

Company/Store name: _____
Website: _____
Userid: _____
Password: _____

Company/Store name: _____
Website: _____
Userid: _____
Password: _____

Company/Store name: _____
Website: _____
Userid: _____
Password: _____

Company/Store name: _____
Website: _____
Userid: _____
Password: _____

Company/Store name: _____
Website: _____
Userid: _____
Password: _____

Company/Store name: _____
Website: _____
Userid: _____
Password: _____

Companies/Businesses

Company/Store name: _____
Website: _____
Userid: _____
Password: _____

Company/Store name: _____
Website: _____
Userid: _____
Password: _____

Company/Store name: _____
Website: _____
Userid: _____
Password: _____

Company/Store name: _____
Website: _____
Userid: _____
Password: _____

Company/Store name: _____
Website: _____
Userid: _____
Password: _____

Company/Store name: _____
Website: _____
Userid: _____
Password: _____

Companies/Businesses F

Company/Store name: _____
Website: _____
Userid: _____
Password: _____

Company/Store name: _____
Website: _____
Userid: _____
Password: _____

Company/Store name: _____
Website: _____
Userid: _____
Password: _____

Company/Store name: _____
Website: _____
Userid: _____
Password: _____

Company/Store name: _____
Website: _____
Userid: _____
Password: _____

Company/Store name: _____
Website: _____
Userid: _____
Password: _____

Companies/Businesses   F

Company/Store name: _____
Website: _____
Userid: _____
Password: _____

Company/Store name: _____
Website: _____
Userid: _____
Password: _____

Company/Store name: _____
Website: _____
Userid: _____
Password: _____

Company/Store name: _____
Website: _____
Userid: _____
Password: _____

Company/Store name: _____
Website: _____
Userid: _____
Password: _____

Company/Store name: _____
Website: _____
Userid: _____
Password: _____

Companies/Businesses

Company/Store name: _____
Website: _____
Userid: _____
Password: _____

Company/Store name: _____
Website: _____
Userid: _____
Password: _____

Company/Store name: _____
Website: _____
Userid: _____
Password: _____

Company/Store name: _____
Website: _____
Userid: _____
Password: _____

Company/Store name: _____
Website: _____
Userid: _____
Password: _____

Company/Store name: _____
Website: _____
Userid: _____
Password: _____

Companies/Businesses

Company/Store name: _____
Website: _____
Userid: _____
Password: _____

Company/Store name: _____
Website: _____
Userid: _____
Password: _____

Company/Store name: _____
Website: _____
Userid: _____
Password: _____

Company/Store name: _____
Website: _____
Userid: _____
Password: _____

Company/Store name: _____
Website: _____
Userid: _____
Password: _____

Company/Store name: _____
Website: _____
Userid: _____
Password: _____

Companies/Businesses

Company/Store name: _____
Website: _____
Userid: _____
Password: _____

Company/Store name: _____
Website: _____
Userid: _____
Password: _____

Company/Store name: _____
Website: _____
Userid: _____
Password: _____

Company/Store name: _____
Website: _____
Userid: _____
Password: _____

Company/Store name: _____
Website: _____
Userid: _____
Password: _____

Company/Store name: _____
Website: _____
Userid: _____
Password: _____

Companies/Businesses

Company/Store name: _____
Website: _____
Userid: _____
Password: _____

Company/Store name: _____
Website: _____
Userid: _____
Password: _____

Company/Store name: _____
Website: _____
Userid: _____
Password: _____

Company/Store name: _____
Website: _____
Userid: _____
Password: _____

Company/Store name: _____
Website: _____
Userid: _____
Password: _____

Company/Store name: _____
Website: _____
Userid: _____
Password: _____

Companies/Businesses ▮

Company/Store name: _____
Website: _____
Userid: _____
Password: _____

Company/Store name: _____
Website: _____
Userid: _____
Password: _____

Company/Store name: _____
Website: _____
Userid: _____
Password: _____

Company/Store name: _____
Website: _____
Userid: _____
Password: _____

Company/Store name: _____
Website: _____
Userid: _____
Password: _____

Company/Store name: _____
Website: _____
Userid: _____
Password: _____

Companies/Businesses

Company/Store name: _____
Website: _____
Userid: _____
Password: _____

Company/Store name: _____
Website: _____
Userid: _____
Password: _____

Company/Store name: _____
Website: _____
Userid: _____
Password: _____

Company/Store name: _____
Website: _____
Userid: _____
Password: _____

Company/Store name: _____
Website: _____
Userid: _____
Password: _____

Company/Store name: _____
Website: _____
Userid: _____
Password: _____

Companies/Businesses

Company/Store name: _____
Website: _____
Userid: _____
Password: _____

Company/Store name: _____
Website: _____
Userid: _____
Password: _____

Company/Store name: _____
Website: _____
Userid: _____
Password: _____

Company/Store name: _____
Website: _____
Userid: _____
Password: _____

Company/Store name: _____
Website: _____
Userid: _____
Password: _____

Company/Store name: _____
Website: _____
Userid: _____
Password: _____

Companies/Businesses

Company/Store name: _____
Website: _____
Userid: _____
Password: _____

Company/Store name: _____
Website: _____
Userid: _____
Password: _____

Company/Store name: _____
Website: _____
Userid: _____
Password: _____

Company/Store name: _____
Website: _____
Userid: _____
Password: _____

Company/Store name: _____
Website: _____
Userid: _____
Password: _____

Company/Store name: _____
Website: _____
Userid: _____
Password: _____

Companies/Businesses

Company/Store name: _____
Website: _____
Userid: _____
Password: _____

Company/Store name: _____
Website: _____
Userid: _____
Password: _____

Company/Store name: _____
Website: _____
Userid: _____
Password: _____

Company/Store name: _____
Website: _____
Userid: _____
Password: _____

Company/Store name: _____
Website: _____
Userid: _____
Password: _____

Company/Store name: _____
Website: _____
Userid: _____
Password: _____

Companies/Businesses

Company/Store name: _____
Website: _____
Userid: _____
Password: _____

Company/Store name: _____
Website: _____
Userid: _____
Password: _____

Company/Store name: _____
Website: _____
Userid: _____
Password: _____

Company/Store name: _____
Website: _____
Userid: _____
Password: _____

Company/Store name: _____
Website: _____
Userid: _____
Password: _____

Company/Store name: _____
Website: _____
Userid: _____
Password: _____

Companies/Businesses

Company/Store name: _____
Website: _____
Userid: _____
Password: _____

Company/Store name: _____
Website: _____
Userid: _____
Password: _____

Company/Store name: _____
Website: _____
Userid: _____
Password: _____

Company/Store name: _____
Website: _____
Userid: _____
Password: _____

Company/Store name: _____
Website: _____
Userid: _____
Password: _____

Company/Store name: _____
Website: _____
Userid: _____
Password: _____

Companies/Businesses

Company/Store name: _____
Website: _____
Userid: _____
Password: _____

Company/Store name: _____
Website: _____
Userid: _____
Password: _____

Company/Store name: _____
Website: _____
Userid: _____
Password: _____

Company/Store name: _____
Website: _____
Userid: _____
Password: _____

Company/Store name: _____
Website: _____
Userid: _____
Password: _____

Company/Store name: _____
Website: _____
Userid: _____
Password: _____

Companies/Businesses

Company/Store name: _____
Website: _____
Userid: _____
Password: _____

Company/Store name: _____
Website: _____
Userid: _____
Password: _____

Company/Store name: _____
Website: _____
Userid: _____
Password: _____

Company/Store name: _____
Website: _____
Userid: _____
Password: _____

Company/Store name: _____
Website: _____
Userid: _____
Password: _____

Company/Store name: _____
Website: _____
Userid: _____
Password: _____

Companies/Businesses

Company/Store name: _____
Website: _____
Userid: _____
Password: _____

Company/Store name: _____
Website: _____
Userid: _____
Password: _____

Company/Store name: _____
Website: _____
Userid: _____
Password: _____

Company/Store name: _____
Website: _____
Userid: _____
Password: _____

Company/Store name: _____
Website: _____
Userid: _____
Password: _____

Company/Store name: _____
Website: _____
Userid: _____
Password: _____

Companies/Businesses

Company/Store name: _____
Website: _____
Userid: _____
Password: _____

Company/Store name: _____
Website: _____
Userid: _____
Password: _____

Company/Store name: _____
Website: _____
Userid: _____
Password: _____

Company/Store name: _____
Website: _____
Userid: _____
Password: _____

Company/Store name: _____
Website: _____
Userid: _____
Password: _____

Company/Store name: _____
Website: _____
Userid: _____
Password: _____

Companies/Businesses

N

Company/Store name: _____
Website: _____
Userid: _____
Password: _____

Company/Store name: _____
Website: _____
Userid: _____
Password: _____

Company/Store name: _____
Website: _____
Userid: _____
Password: _____

Company/Store name: _____
Website: _____
Userid: _____
Password: _____

Company/Store name: _____
Website: _____
Userid: _____
Password: _____

Company/Store name: _____
Website: _____
Userid: _____
Password: _____

Companies/Businesses

Company/Store name: _____
Website: _____
Userid: _____
Password: _____

Company/Store name: _____
Website: _____
Userid: _____
Password: _____

Company/Store name: _____
Website: _____
Userid: _____
Password: _____

Company/Store name: _____
Website: _____
Userid: _____
Password: _____

Company/Store name: _____
Website: _____
Userid: _____
Password: _____

Company/Store name: _____
Website: _____
Userid: _____
Password: _____

Companies/Businesses

Company/Store name: _____
Website: _____
Userid: _____
Password: _____

Company/Store name: _____
Website: _____
Userid: _____
Password: _____

Company/Store name: _____
Website: _____
Userid: _____
Password: _____

Company/Store name: _____
Website: _____
Userid: _____
Password: _____

Company/Store name: _____
Website: _____
Userid: _____
Password: _____

Company/Store name: _____
Website: _____
Userid: _____
Password: _____

Companies/Businesses

Company/Store name: _____
Website: _____
Userid: _____
Password: _____

Company/Store name: _____
Website: _____
Userid: _____
Password: _____

Company/Store name: _____
Website: _____
Userid: _____
Password: _____

Company/Store name: _____
Website: _____
Userid: _____
Password: _____

Company/Store name: _____
Website: _____
Userid: _____
Password: _____

Company/Store name: _____
Website: _____
Userid: _____
Password: _____

Companies/Businesses

Company/Store name: _____
Website: _____
Userid: _____
Password: _____

Company/Store name: _____
Website: _____
Userid: _____
Password: _____

Company/Store name: _____
Website: _____
Userid: _____
Password: _____

Company/Store name: _____
Website: _____
Userid: _____
Password: _____

Company/Store name: _____
Website: _____
Userid: _____
Password: _____

Company/Store name: _____
Website: _____
Userid: _____
Password: _____

Companies/Businesses

Company/Store name: _____
Website: _____
Userid: _____
Password: _____

Company/Store name: _____
Website: _____
Userid: _____
Password: _____

Company/Store name: _____
Website: _____
Userid: _____
Password: _____

Company/Store name: _____
Website: _____
Userid: _____
Password: _____

Company/Store name: _____
Website: _____
Userid: _____
Password: _____

Company/Store name: _____
Website: _____
Userid: _____
Password: _____

Companies/Businesses

Q

Company/Store name: _____
Website: _____
Userid: _____
Password: _____

Company/Store name: _____
Website: _____
Userid: _____
Password: _____

Company/Store name: _____
Website: _____
Userid: _____
Password: _____

Company/Store name: _____
Website: _____
Userid: _____
Password: _____

Company/Store name: _____
Website: _____
Userid: _____
Password: _____

Company/Store name: _____
Website: _____
Userid: _____
Password: _____

Companies/Businesses

Company/Store name: _____
Website: _____
Userid: _____
Password: _____

Company/Store name: _____
Website: _____
Userid: _____
Password: _____

Company/Store name: _____
Website: _____
Userid: _____
Password: _____

Company/Store name: _____
Website: _____
Userid: _____
Password: _____

Company/Store name: _____
Website: _____
Userid: _____
Password: _____

Company/Store name: _____
Website: _____
Userid: _____
Password: _____

Companies/Businesses

Company/Store name: _____
Website: _____
Userid: _____
Password: _____

Company/Store name: _____
Website: _____
Userid: _____
Password: _____

Company/Store name: _____
Website: _____
Userid: _____
Password: _____

Company/Store name: _____
Website: _____
Userid: _____
Password: _____

Company/Store name: _____
Website: _____
Userid: _____
Password: _____

Company/Store name: _____
Website: _____
Userid: _____
Password: _____

Companies/Businesses

Company/Store name: _____
Website: _____
Userid: _____
Password: _____

Company/Store name: _____
Website: _____
Userid: _____
Password: _____

Company/Store name: _____
Website: _____
Userid: _____
Password: _____

Company/Store name: _____
Website: _____
Userid: _____
Password: _____

Company/Store name: _____
Website: _____
Userid: _____
Password: _____

Company/Store name: _____
Website: _____
Userid: _____
Password: _____

Companies/Businesses

Company/Store name: _____
Website: _____
Userid: _____
Password: _____

Company/Store name: _____
Website: _____
Userid: _____
Password: _____

Company/Store name: _____
Website: _____
Userid: _____
Password: _____

Company/Store name: _____
Website: _____
Userid: _____
Password: _____

Company/Store name: _____
Website: _____
Userid: _____
Password: _____

Company/Store name: _____
Website: _____
Userid: _____
Password: _____

Companies/Businesses

Company/Store name: _____
Website: _____
Userid: _____
Password: _____

Company/Store name: _____
Website: _____
Userid: _____
Password: _____

Company/Store name: _____
Website: _____
Userid: _____
Password: _____

Company/Store name: _____
Website: _____
Userid: _____
Password: _____

Company/Store name: _____
Website: _____
Userid: _____
Password: _____

Company/Store name: _____
Website: _____
Userid: _____
Password: _____

Companies/Businesses

Company/Store name: _____
Website: _____
Userid: _____
Password: _____

Company/Store name: _____
Website: _____
Userid: _____
Password: _____

Company/Store name: _____
Website: _____
Userid: _____
Password: _____

Company/Store name: _____
Website: _____
Userid: _____
Password: _____

Company/Store name: _____
Website: _____
Userid: _____
Password: _____

Company/Store name: _____
Website: _____
Userid: _____
Password: _____

Companies/Businesses

Company/Store name: _____
Website: _____
Userid: _____
Password: _____

Company/Store name: _____
Website: _____
Userid: _____
Password: _____

Company/Store name: _____
Website: _____
Userid: _____
Password: _____

Company/Store name: _____
Website: _____
Userid: _____
Password: _____

Company/Store name: _____
Website: _____
Userid: _____
Password: _____

Company/Store name: _____
Website: _____
Userid: _____
Password: _____

Companies/Businesses

Company/Store name: _____
Website: _____
Userid: _____
Password: _____

Company/Store name: _____
Website: _____
Userid: _____
Password: _____

Company/Store name: _____
Website: _____
Userid: _____
Password: _____

Company/Store name: _____
Website: _____
Userid: _____
Password: _____

Company/Store name: _____
Website: _____
Userid: _____
Password: _____

Company/Store name: _____
Website: _____
Userid: _____
Password: _____

Companies/Businesses

V

Company/Store name: _____
Website: _____
Userid: _____
Password: _____

Company/Store name: _____
Website: _____
Userid: _____
Password: _____

Company/Store name: _____
Website: _____
Userid: _____
Password: _____

Company/Store name: _____
Website: _____
Userid: _____
Password: _____

Company/Store name: _____
Website: _____
Userid: _____
Password: _____

Company/Store name: _____
Website: _____
Userid: _____
Password: _____

Companies/Businesses

Company/Store name: _____
Website: _____
Userid: _____
Password: _____

Company/Store name: _____
Website: _____
Userid: _____
Password: _____

Company/Store name: _____
Website: _____
Userid: _____
Password: _____

Company/Store name: _____
Website: _____
Userid: _____
Password: _____

Company/Store name: _____
Website: _____
Userid: _____
Password: _____

Company/Store name: _____
Website: _____
Userid: _____
Password: _____

Companies/Businesses

Company/Store name: _____
Website: _____
Userid: _____
Password: _____

Company/Store name: _____
Website: _____
Userid: _____
Password: _____

Company/Store name: _____
Website: _____
Userid: _____
Password: _____

Company/Store name: _____
Website: _____
Userid: _____
Password: _____

Company/Store name: _____
Website: _____
Userid: _____
Password: _____

Company/Store name: _____
Website: _____
Userid: _____
Password: _____

Companies/Businesses

W

Company/Store name: _____
Website: _____
Userid: _____
Password: _____

Company/Store name: _____
Website: _____
Userid: _____
Password: _____

Company/Store name: _____
Website: _____
Userid: _____
Password: _____

Company/Store name: _____
Website: _____
Userid: _____
Password: _____

Company/Store name: _____
Website: _____
Userid: _____
Password: _____

Company/Store name: _____
Website: _____
Userid: _____
Password: _____

Companies/Businesses

Company/Store name: _____
Website: _____
Userid: _____
Password: _____

Company/Store name: _____
Website: _____
Userid: _____
Password: _____

Company/Store name: _____
Website: _____
Userid: _____
Password: _____

Company/Store name: _____
Website: _____
Userid: _____
Password: _____

Company/Store name: _____
Website: _____
Userid: _____
Password: _____

Company/Store name: _____
Website: _____
Userid: _____
Password: _____

Companies/Businesses

Company/Store name: _____
Website: _____
Userid: _____
Password: _____

Company/Store name: _____
Website: _____
Userid: _____
Password: _____

Company/Store name: _____
Website: _____
Userid: _____
Password: _____

Company/Store name: _____
Website: _____
Userid: _____
Password: _____

Company/Store name: _____
Website: _____
Userid: _____
Password: _____

Company/Store name: _____
Website: _____
Userid: _____
Password: _____

Companies/Businesses

Y

Company/Store name: _____
Website: _____
Userid: _____
Password: _____

Company/Store name: _____
Website: _____
Userid: _____
Password: _____

Company/Store name: _____
Website: _____
Userid: _____
Password: _____

Company/Store name: _____
Website: _____
Userid: _____
Password: _____

Company/Store name: _____
Website: _____
Userid: _____
Password: _____

Company/Store name: _____
Website: _____
Userid: _____
Password: _____

Companies/Businesses

Company/Store name: _____
Website: _____
Userid: _____
Password: _____

Company/Store name: _____
Website: _____
Userid: _____
Password: _____

Company/Store name: _____
Website: _____
Userid: _____
Password: _____

Company/Store name: _____
Website: _____
Userid: _____
Password: _____

Company/Store name: _____
Website: _____
Userid: _____
Password: _____

Company/Store name: _____
Website: _____
Userid: _____
Password: _____

Companies/Businesses

Company/Store name: _____
Website: _____
Userid: _____
Password: _____

Company/Store name: _____
Website: _____
Userid: _____
Password: _____

Company/Store name: _____
Website: _____
Userid: _____
Password: _____

Company/Store name: _____
Website: _____
Userid: _____
Password: _____

Company/Store name: _____
Website: _____
Userid: _____
Password: _____

Company/Store name: _____
Website: _____
Userid: _____
Password: _____

Banks/Financial Institutions A/B

Bank Name: _____
Userid: _____
Password: _____
Security Code: _____
Account #: _____

Bank Name: _____
Userid: _____
Password: _____
Security Code: _____
Account #: _____

Bank Name: _____
Userid: _____
Password: _____
Security Code: _____
Account #: _____

Bank Name: _____
Userid: _____
Password: _____
Security Code: _____
Account #: _____

Bank Name: _____
Userid: _____
Password: _____
Security Code: _____
Account #: _____

Bank Name: _____
Userid: _____
Password: _____
Security Code: _____
Account #: _____

Bank Name: _____
Userid: _____
Password: _____
Security Code: _____
Account #: _____

Banks/Financial Institutions A/B

Bank Name: _____
Userid: _____
Password: _____
Security Code: _____
Account #: _____

Bank Name: _____
Userid: _____
Password: _____
Security Code: _____
Account #: _____

Bank Name: _____
Userid: _____
Password: _____
Security Code: _____
Account #: _____

Bank Name: _____
Userid: _____
Password: _____
Security Code: _____
Account #: _____

Bank Name: _____
Userid: _____
Password: _____
Security Code: _____
Account #: _____

Bank Name: _____
Userid: _____
Password: _____
Security Code: _____
Account #: _____

Banks/Financial Institutions   C/D

Bank Name: _____
Userid: _____
Password: _____
Security Code: _____
Account #: _____

Bank Name: _____
Userid: _____
Password: _____
Security Code: _____
Account #: _____

Bank Name: _____
Userid: _____
Password: _____
Security Code: _____
Account #: _____

Bank Name: _____
Userid: _____
Password: _____
Security Code: _____
Account #: _____

Bank Name: _____
Userid: _____
Password: _____
Security Code: _____
Account #: _____

Bank Name: _____
Userid: _____
Password: _____
Security Code: _____
Account #: _____

Banks/Financial Institutions   C/D

Bank Name: _____
Userid: _____
Password: _____
Security Code: _____
Account #: _____

Bank Name: _____
Userid: _____
Password: _____
Security Code: _____
Account #: _____

Bank Name: _____
Userid: _____
Password: _____
Security Code: _____
Account #: _____

Bank Name: _____
Userid: _____
Password: _____
Security Code: _____
Account #: _____

Bank Name: _____
Userid: _____
Password: _____
Security Code: _____
Account #: _____

Bank Name: _____
Userid: _____
Password: _____
Security Code: _____
Account #: _____

Banks/Financial Institutions   E/F

Bank Name: _____
Userid: _____
Password: _____
Security Code: _____
Account #: _____

Bank Name: _____
Userid: _____
Password: _____
Security Code: _____
Account #: _____

Bank Name: _____
Userid: _____
Password: _____
Security Code: _____
Account #: _____

Bank Name: _____
Userid: _____
Password: _____
Security Code: _____
Account #: _____

Bank Name: _____
Userid: _____
Password: _____
Security Code: _____
Account #: _____

Bank Name: _____
Userid: _____
Password: _____
Security Code: _____
Account #: _____

Banks/Financial Institutions   E/F

Bank Name: _____
Userid: _____
Password: _____
Security Code: _____
Account #: _____

Bank Name: _____
Userid: _____
Password: _____
Security Code: _____
Account #: _____

Bank Name: _____
Userid: _____
Password: _____
Security Code: _____
Account #: _____

Bank Name: _____
Userid: _____
Password: _____
Security Code: _____
Account #: _____

Bank Name: _____
Userid: _____
Password: _____
Security Code: _____
Account #: _____

Bank Name: _____
Userid: _____
Password: _____
Security Code: _____
Account #: _____

Banks/Financial Institutions   G/H

Bank Name: _____
Userid: _____
Password: _____
Security Code: _____
Account #: _____

Bank Name: _____
Userid: _____
Password: _____
Security Code: _____
Account #: _____

Bank Name: _____
Userid: _____
Password: _____
Security Code: _____
Account #: _____

Bank Name: _____
Userid: _____
Password: _____
Security Code: _____
Account #: _____

Bank Name: _____
Userid: _____
Password: _____
Security Code: _____
Account #: _____

Bank Name: _____
Userid: _____
Password: _____
Security Code: _____
Account #: _____

Banks/Financial Institutions   G/H

Bank Name: _____
Userid: _____
Password: _____
Security Code: _____
Account #: _____

Bank Name: _____
Userid: _____
Password: _____
Security Code: _____
Account #: _____

Bank Name: _____
Userid: _____
Password: _____
Security Code: _____
Account #: _____

Bank Name: _____
Userid: _____
Password: _____
Security Code: _____
Account #: _____

Bank Name: _____
Userid: _____
Password: _____
Security Code: _____
Account #: _____

Bank Name: _____
Userid: _____
Password: _____
Security Code: _____
Account #: _____

Banks/Financial Institutions   I/J

Bank Name: _____
Userid: _____
Password: _____
Security Code: _____
Account #: _____

Bank Name: _____
Userid: _____
Password: _____
Security Code: _____
Account #: _____

Bank Name: _____
Userid: _____
Password: _____
Security Code: _____
Account #: _____

Bank Name: _____
Userid: _____
Password: _____
Security Code: _____
Account #: _____

Bank Name: _____
Userid: _____
Password: _____
Security Code: _____
Account #: _____

Bank Name: _____
Userid: _____
Password: _____
Security Code: _____
Account #: _____

Banks/Financial Institutions   I/J

Bank Name: _____
Userid: _____
Password: _____
Security Code: _____
Account #: _____

Bank Name: _____
Userid: _____
Password: _____
Security Code: _____
Account #: _____

Bank Name: _____
Userid: _____
Password: _____
Security Code: _____
Account #: _____

Bank Name: _____
Userid: _____
Password: _____
Security Code: _____
Account #: _____

Bank Name: _____
Userid: _____
Password: _____
Security Code: _____
Account #: _____

Bank Name: _____
Userid: _____
Password: _____
Security Code: _____
Account #: _____

Banks/Financial Institutions K/L

Bank Name: _____
Userid: _____
Password: _____
Security Code: _____
Account #: _____

Bank Name: _____
Userid: _____
Password: _____
Security Code: _____
Account #: _____

Bank Name: _____
Userid: _____
Password: _____
Security Code: _____
Account #: _____

Bank Name: _____
Userid: _____
Password: _____
Security Code: _____
Account #: _____

Bank Name: _____
Userid: _____
Password: _____
Security Code: _____
Account #: _____

Bank Name: _____
Userid: _____
Password: _____
Security Code: _____
Account #: _____

Banks/Financial Institutions   K/L

Bank Name: _____
Userid: _____
Password: _____
Security Code: _____
Account #: _____

Bank Name: _____
Userid: _____
Password: _____
Security Code: _____
Account #: _____

Bank Name: _____
Userid: _____
Password: _____
Security Code: _____
Account #: _____

Bank Name: _____
Userid: _____
Password: _____
Security Code: _____
Account #: _____

Bank Name: _____
Userid: _____
Password: _____
Security Code: _____
Account #: _____

Bank Name: _____
Userid: _____
Password: _____
Security Code: _____
Account #: _____

Bank Name: _____
Userid: _____
Password: _____
Security Code: _____
Account #: _____

Banks/Financial Institutions   M/N

Bank Name:
Userid:
Password:
Security Code:
Account #:

Bank Name:
Userid:
Password:
Security Code:
Account #:

Bank Name:
Userid:
Password:
Security Code:
Account #:

Bank Name:
Userid:
Password:
Security Code:
Account #:

Bank Name:
Userid:
Password:
Security Code:
Account #:

Bank Name:
Userid:
Password:
Security Code:
Account #:

Banks/Financial Institutions   M/N

Bank Name: _____
Userid: _____
Password: _____
Security Code: _____
Account #: _____

Bank Name: _____
Userid: _____
Password: _____
Security Code: _____
Account #: _____

Bank Name: _____
Userid: _____
Password: _____
Security Code: _____
Account #: _____

Bank Name: _____
Userid: _____
Password: _____
Security Code: _____
Account #: _____

Bank Name: _____
Userid: _____
Password: _____
Security Code: _____
Account #: _____

Bank Name: _____
Userid: _____
Password: _____
Security Code: _____
Account #: _____

Banks/Financial Institutions   O/P

Bank Name: _____
Userid: _____
Password: _____
Security Code: _____
Account #: _____

Bank Name: _____
Userid: _____
Password: _____
Security Code: _____
Account #: _____

Bank Name: _____
Userid: _____
Password: _____
Security Code: _____
Account #: _____

Bank Name: _____
Userid: _____
Password: _____
Security Code: _____
Account #: _____

Bank Name: _____
Userid: _____
Password: _____
Security Code: _____
Account #: _____

Bank Name: _____
Userid: _____
Password: _____
Security Code: _____
Account #: _____

Bank Name: _____
Userid: _____
Password: _____
Security Code: _____
Account #: _____

Banks/Financial Institutions   O/P

Bank Name: _____
Userid: _____
Password: _____
Security Code: _____
Account #: _____

Bank Name: _____
Userid: _____
Password: _____
Security Code: _____
Account #: _____

Bank Name: _____
Userid: _____
Password: _____
Security Code: _____
Account #: _____

Bank Name: _____
Userid: _____
Password: _____
Security Code: _____
Account #: _____

Bank Name: _____
Userid: _____
Password: _____
Security Code: _____
Account #: _____

Bank Name: _____
Userid: _____
Password: _____
Security Code: _____
Account #: _____

Banks/Financial Institutions   Q/R

Bank Name: _____
Userid: _____
Password: _____
Security Code: _____
Account #: _____

Bank Name: _____
Userid: _____
Password: _____
Security Code: _____
Account #: _____

Bank Name: _____
Userid: _____
Password: _____
Security Code: _____
Account #: _____

Bank Name: _____
Userid: _____
Password: _____
Security Code: _____
Account #: _____

Bank Name: _____
Userid: _____
Password: _____
Security Code: _____
Account #: _____

Bank Name: _____
Userid: _____
Password: _____
Security Code: _____
Account #: _____

Banks/Financial Institutions   Q/R

Bank Name: _____
Userid: _____
Password: _____
Security Code: _____
Account #: _____

Bank Name: _____
Userid: _____
Password: _____
Security Code: _____
Account #: _____

Bank Name: _____
Userid: _____
Password: _____
Security Code: _____
Account #: _____

Bank Name: _____
Userid: _____
Password: _____
Security Code: _____
Account #: _____

Bank Name: _____
Userid: _____
Password: _____
Security Code: _____
Account #: _____

Bank Name: _____
Userid: _____
Password: _____
Security Code: _____
Account #: _____

Banks/Financial Institutions   S/T

Bank Name: _____
Userid: _____
Password: _____
Security Code: _____
Account #: _____

Bank Name: _____
Userid: _____
Password: _____
Security Code: _____
Account #: _____

Bank Name: _____
Userid: _____
Password: _____
Security Code: _____
Account #: _____

Bank Name: _____
Userid: _____
Password: _____
Security Code: _____
Account #: _____

Bank Name: _____
Userid: _____
Password: _____
Security Code: _____
Account #: _____

Bank Name: _____
Userid: _____
Password: _____
Security Code: _____
Account #: _____

Banks/Financial Institutions   S/T

Bank Name: _____
Userid: _____
Password: _____
Security Code: _____
Account #: _____

Bank Name: _____
Userid: _____
Password: _____
Security Code: _____
Account #: _____

Bank Name: _____
Userid: _____
Password: _____
Security Code: _____
Account #: _____

Bank Name: _____
Userid: _____
Password: _____
Security Code: _____
Account #: _____

Bank Name: _____
Userid: _____
Password: _____
Security Code: _____
Account #: _____

Bank Name: _____
Userid: _____
Password: _____
Security Code: _____
Account #: _____

Banks/Financial Institutions   U/V

Bank Name: _____
Userid: _____
Password: _____
Security Code: _____
Account #: _____

Bank Name: _____
Userid: _____
Password: _____
Security Code: _____
Account #: _____

Bank Name: _____
Userid: _____
Password: _____
Security Code: _____
Account #: _____

Bank Name: _____
Userid: _____
Password: _____
Security Code: _____
Account #: _____

Bank Name: _____
Userid: _____
Password: _____
Security Code: _____
Account #: _____

Bank Name: _____
Userid: _____
Password: _____
Security Code: _____
Account #: _____

Banks/Financial Institutions   U/V

Bank Name: _____
Userid: _____
Password: _____
Security Code: _____
Account #: _____

Bank Name: _____
Userid: _____
Password: _____
Security Code: _____
Account #: _____

Bank Name: _____
Userid: _____
Password: _____
Security Code: _____
Account #: _____

Bank Name: _____
Userid: _____
Password: _____
Security Code: _____
Account #: _____

Bank Name: _____
Userid: _____
Password: _____
Security Code: _____
Account #: _____

Bank Name: _____
Userid: _____
Password: _____
Security Code: _____
Account #: _____

Banks/Financial Institutions   W/X

Bank Name: _____
Userid: _____
Password: _____
Security Code: _____
Account #: _____

Bank Name: _____
Userid: _____
Password: _____
Security Code: _____
Account #: _____

Bank Name: _____
Userid: _____
Password: _____
Security Code: _____
Account #: _____

Bank Name: _____
Userid: _____
Password: _____
Security Code: _____
Account #: _____

Bank Name: _____
Userid: _____
Password: _____
Security Code: _____
Account #: _____

Bank Name: _____
Userid: _____
Password: _____
Security Code: _____
Account #: _____

Banks/Financial Institutions   W/X

Bank Name: _____
Userid: _____
Password: _____
Security Code: _____
Account #: _____

Bank Name: _____
Userid: _____
Password: _____
Security Code: _____
Account #: _____

Bank Name: _____
Userid: _____
Password: _____
Security Code: _____
Account #: _____

Bank Name: _____
Userid: _____
Password: _____
Security Code: _____
Account #: _____

Bank Name: _____
Userid: _____
Password: _____
Security Code: _____
Account #: _____

Bank Name: _____
Userid: _____
Password: _____
Security Code: _____
Account #: _____

Banks/Financial Institutions   Y/Z

Bank Name: _____
Userid: _____
Password: _____
Security Code: _____
Account #: _____

Bank Name: _____
Userid: _____
Password: _____
Security Code: _____
Account #: _____

Bank Name: _____
Userid: _____
Password: _____
Security Code: _____
Account #: _____

Bank Name: _____
Userid: _____
Password: _____
Security Code: _____
Account #: _____

Bank Name: _____
Userid: _____
Password: _____
Security Code: _____
Account #: _____

Bank Name: _____
Userid: _____
Password: _____
Security Code: _____
Account #: _____

Banks/Financial Institutions   Y/Z

Bank Name: _____
Userid: _____
Password: _____
Security Code: _____
Account #: _____

Bank Name: _____
Userid: _____
Password: _____
Security Code: _____
Account #: _____

Bank Name: _____
Userid: _____
Password: _____
Security Code: _____
Account #: _____

Bank Name: _____
Userid: _____
Password: _____
Security Code: _____
Account #: _____

Bank Name: _____
Userid: _____
Password: _____
Security Code: _____
Account #: _____

Bank Name: _____
Userid: _____
Password: _____
Security Code: _____
Account #: _____

E-Mail Addresses

Name:
E-mail address:

Name:
E-mail address:

Name:
E-mail address:

Name:
E-mail address:

Name:
E-mail address:

Name:
E-mail address:

Name:
E-mail address:

Name:
E-mail address:

Name:
E-mail address:

Name:
E-mail address:

Name:
E-mail address:

Name:
E-mail address:

E-Mail Addresses

Name: _____
E-mail address: _____

Name: _____
E-mail address: _____

Name: _____
E-mail address: _____

Name: _____
E-mail address: _____

Name: _____
E-mail address: _____

Name: _____
E-mail address: _____

Name: _____
E-mail address: _____

Name: _____
E-mail address: _____

Name: _____
E-mail address: _____

Name: _____
E-mail address: _____

Name: _____
E-mail address: _____

Name: _____
E-mail address: _____

E-Mail Addresses

Name:
E-mail address:

Name:
E-mail address:

Name:
E-mail address:

Name:
E-mail address:

Name:
E-mail address:

Name:
E-mail address:

Name:
E-mail address:

Name:
E-mail address:

Name:
E-mail address:

Name:
E-mail address:

Name:
E-mail address:

Name:
E-mail address:

E-Mail Addresses

Name: _____
E-mail address: _____

Name: _____
E-mail address: _____

Name: _____
E-mail address: _____

Name: _____
E-mail address: _____

Name: _____
E-mail address: _____

Name: _____
E-mail address: _____

Name: _____
E-mail address: _____

Name: _____
E-mail address: _____

Name: _____
E-mail address: _____

Name: _____
E-mail address: _____

Name: _____
E-mail address: _____

Name: _____
E-mail address: _____

E-Mail Addresses

Name:
E-mail address:

Name:
E-mail address:

Name:
E-mail address:

Name:
E-mail address:

Name:
E-mail address:

Name:
E-mail address:

Name:
E-mail address:

Name:
E-mail address:

Name:
E-mail address:

Name:
E-mail address:

Name:
E-mail address:

Name:
E-mail address:

E-Mail Addresses

Name:
E-mail address: _____

Name:
E-mail address: _____

Name:
E-mail address: _____

Name:
E-mail address: _____

Name:
E-mail address: _____

Name:
E-mail address: _____

Name:
E-mail address: _____

Name:
E-mail address: _____

Name:
E-mail address: _____

Name:
E-mail address: _____

Name:
E-mail address: _____

Name:
E-mail address: _____

E-Mail Addresses

Name:
E-mail address:

Name:
E-mail address:

Name:
E-mail address:

Name:
E-mail address:

Name:
E-mail address:

Name:
E-mail address:

Name:
E-mail address:

Name:
E-mail address:

Name:
E-mail address:

Name:
E-mail address:

Name:
E-mail address:

Name:
E-mail address:

E-Mail Addresses

Name:
E-mail address:

Name:
E-mail address:

Name:
E-mail address:

Name:
E-mail address:

Name:
E-mail address:

Name:
E-mail address:

Name:
E-mail address:

Name:
E-mail address:

Name:
E-mail address:

Name:
E-mail address:

Name:
E-mail address:

E-Mail Addresses

Name:
E-mail address:

Name:
E-mail address:

Name:
E-mail address:

Name:
E-mail address:

Name:
E-mail address:

Name:
E-mail address:

Name:
E-mail address:

Name:
E-mail address:

Name:
E-mail address:

Name:
E-mail address:

Name:
E-mail address:

Name:
E-mail address:

E-Mail Addresses

Name: _____
E-mail address: _____

Name: _____
E-mail address: _____

Name: _____
E-mail address: _____

Name: _____
E-mail address: _____

Name: _____
E-mail address: _____

Name: _____
E-mail address: _____

Name: _____
E-mail address: _____

Name: _____
E-mail address: _____

Name: _____
E-mail address: _____

Name: _____
E-mail address: _____

Name: _____
E-mail address: _____

Name: _____
E-mail address: _____

E-Mail Addresses

Name:
E-mail address:

Name:
E-mail address:

Name:
E-mail address:

Name:
E-mail address:

Name:
E-mail address:

Name:
E-mail address:

Name:
E-mail address:

Name:
E-mail address:

Name:
E-mail address:

Name:
E-mail address:

Name:
E-mail address:

Name:
E-mail address:

E-Mail Addresses

Name:
E-mail address:

Name:
E-mail address:

Name:
E-mail address:

Name:
E-mail address:

Name:
E-mail address:

Name:
E-mail address:

Name:
E-mail address:

Name:
E-mail address:

Name:
E-mail address:

Name:
E-mail address:

Name:
E-mail address:

Name:
E-mail address:

E-Mail Addresses

Name:
E-mail address:

Name:
E-mail address:

Name:
E-mail address:

Name:
E-mail address:

Name:
E-mail address:

Name:
E-mail address:

Name:
E-mail address:

Name:
E-mail address:

Name:
E-mail address:

Name:
E-mail address:

Name:
E-mail address:

Name:
E-mail address:

E-Mail Addresses

Name:
E-mail address:

Name:
E-mail address:

Name:
E-mail address:

Name:
E-mail address:

Name:
E-mail address:

Name:
E-mail address:

Name:
E-mail address:

Name:
E-mail address:

Name:
E-mail address:

Name:
E-mail address:

Name:
E-mail address:

Name:
E-mail address:

E-Mail Addresses

Name:
E-mail address: _____

Name:
E-mail address: _____

Name:
E-mail address: _____

Name:
E-mail address: _____

Name:
E-mail address: _____

Name:
E-mail address: _____

Name:
E-mail address: _____

Name:
E-mail address: _____

Name:
E-mail address: _____

Name:
E-mail address: _____

Name:
E-mail address: _____

Name:
E-mail address: _____

E-Mail Addresses

Name: _____
E-mail address: _____

Name: _____
E-mail address: _____

Name: _____
E-mail address: _____

Name: _____
E-mail address: _____

Name: _____
E-mail address: _____

Name: _____
E-mail address: _____

Name: _____
E-mail address: _____

Name: _____
E-mail address: _____

Name: _____
E-mail address: _____

Name: _____
E-mail address: _____

Name: _____
E-mail address: _____

Name: _____
E-mail address: _____

E-Mail Addresses

Name: _____
E-mail address: _____

Name: _____
E-mail address: _____

Name: _____
E-mail address: _____

Name: _____
E-mail address: _____

Name: _____
E-mail address: _____

Name: _____
E-mail address: _____

Name: _____
E-mail address: _____

Name: _____
E-mail address: _____

Name: _____
E-mail address: _____

Name: _____
E-mail address: _____

Name: _____
E-mail address: _____

Name: _____
E-mail address: _____

E-Mail Addresses

Name:
E-mail address: _____

Name:
E-mail address: _____

Name:
E-mail address: _____

Name:
E-mail address: _____

Name:
E-mail address: _____

Name:
E-mail address: _____

Name:
E-mail address: _____

Name:
E-mail address: _____

Name:
E-mail address: _____

Name:
E-mail address: _____

Name:
E-mail address: _____

Name:
E-mail address: _____

E-Mail Addresses

Name: _____
E-mail address: _____

Name: _____
E-mail address: _____

Name: _____
E-mail address: _____

Name: _____
E-mail address: _____

Name: _____
E-mail address: _____

Name: _____
E-mail address: _____

Name: _____
E-mail address: _____

Name: _____
E-mail address: _____

Name: _____
E-mail address: _____

Name: _____
E-mail address: _____

Name: _____
E-mail address: _____

Name: _____
E-mail address: _____

E-Mail Addresses

Name:
E-mail address: _____

Name:
E-mail address: _____

Name:
E-mail address: _____

Name:
E-mail address: _____

Name:
E-mail address: _____

Name:
E-mail address: _____

Name:
E-mail address: _____

Name:
E-mail address: _____

Name:
E-mail address: _____

Name:
E-mail address: _____

Name:
E-mail address: _____

Name:
E-mail address: _____

E-Mail Addresses

U/V

Name:
E-mail address: _____

Name:
E-mail address: _____

Name:
E-mail address: _____

Name:
E-mail address: _____

Name:
E-mail address: _____

Name:
E-mail address: _____

Name:
E-mail address: _____

Name:
E-mail address: _____

Name:
E-mail address: _____

Name:
E-mail address: _____

Name:
E-mail address: _____

Name:
E-mail address: _____

E-Mail Addresses

Name: \
E-mail address: _____

Name: \
E-mail address: _____

Name: \
E-mail address: _____

Name: \
E-mail address: _____

Name: \
E-mail address: _____

Name: \
E-mail address: _____

Name: \
E-mail address: _____

Name: \
E-mail address: _____

Name: \
E-mail address: _____

Name: \
E-mail address: _____

Name: \
E-mail address: _____

Name: \
E-mail address: _____

E-Mail Addresses

Name:
E-mail address:

Name:
E-mail address:

Name:
E-mail address:

Name:
E-mail address:

Name:
E-mail address:

Name:
E-mail address:

Name:
E-mail address:

Name:
E-mail address:

Name:
E-mail address:

Name:
E-mail address:

Name:
E-mail address:

Name:
E-mail address:

E-Mail Addresses

Name:
E-mail address:

Name:
E-mail address:

Name:
E-mail address:

Name:
E-mail address:

Name:
E-mail address:

Name:
E-mail address:

Name:
E-mail address:

Name:
E-mail address:

Name:
E-mail address:

Name:
E-mail address:

Name:
E-mail address:

Name:
E-mail address:

E-Mail Addresses

Name: _____
E-mail address: _____

Name: _____
E-mail address: _____

Name: _____
E-mail address: _____

Name: _____
E-mail address: _____

Name: _____
E-mail address: _____

Name: _____
E-mail address: _____

Name: _____
E-mail address: _____

Name: _____
E-mail address: _____

Name: _____
E-mail address: _____

Name: _____
E-mail address: _____

Name: _____
E-mail address: _____

Name: _____
E-mail address: _____

E-Mail Addresses

Name:
E-mail address:

Name:
E-mail address:

Name:
E-mail address:

Name:
E-mail address:

Name:
E-mail address:

Name:
E-mail address:

Name:
E-mail address:

Name:
E-mail address:

Name:
E-mail address:

Name:
E-mail address:

Name:
E-mail address:

Name:
E-mail address: